Life Story of a
Frog

Charlotte Guillain

raintree

a Capstone company — publishers for children

Raintree is an imprint of Capstone Global Library Limited, a company incorporated in England and Wales having its registered office at 7 Pilgrim Street, London, EC4V 6LB – Registered company number: 6695582

www.raintreepublishers.co.uk
myorders@raintreepublishers.co.uk

Text © Capstone Global Library Limited 2015
First published in hardback 2014
Published in paperback in 2015
The moral rights of the proprietor have been asserted.

Edited by Catherine Veitch and Gina Kammer
Designed by Richard Parker and Peggie Carley
Picture research by Mica Brancic
Production by Victoria Fitzgerald
Originated by Capstone Global Library Ltd
Printed and bound in China by Leo Paper Group

ISBN 978 1 406 28234 4 (hardback)
18 17 16 15 14
10 9 8 7 6 5 4 3 2 1

ISBN 978 1 406 28239 9 (paperback)
19 18 17 16 15
10 9 8 7 6 5 4 3 2

British Library Cataloguing in Publication Data
A full catalogue record for this book is available from the British Library.

Acknowledgements
We would like to thank the following for permission to reproduce photographs:

Dreamstime: Marcelkudla, 18; FLPA: David Tipling, 4, 9, Minden Pictures/Cyril Ruoso, 23, Minden Pictures/Thomas Marent, 14, 15, Paul Hobson, 25, Richard Becker, 8, 10, Tony Hamblin, 27; Getty Images: Roland Bogush, cover; Minden Pictures: Foto Natura/Rene Krekels, 17, Wil Meinderts, 11; Science Source: Francoise Sauze, 24, G. I. Bernard, 13, Robert Henno, 22, Stephen Dalton, 12; Shutterstock: AlexussK (stone design element), cover and throughout, Arto Hakola, 16, Birute Vijeikiene, 7, Dirk Ercken, 19, Eric Isselee, 28, 29, jannoon028 (grass border), throughout, Yuliya Proskurina (green leaves border), cover and throughout, Zuzule, 6; SuperStock: F1 Online/F Rauschenbach, 20, Mauritius/Herbert Kehrer, 5, NHPA, 21, 26

We would like to thank Michael Bright for his assistance in the preparation of this book.

Every effort has been made to contact copyright holders of material reproduced in this book. Any omissions will be rectified in subsequent printings if notice is given to the publisher.

Contents

Some words are shown in bold, **like this**. You can find out what they mean by looking in the glossary.

What is a frog?

A frog is a type of animal called an **amphibian**. Amphibians are animals with backbones that can live on land and in water. All amphibians have soft, damp skin.

There are many types of frogs. They can live in many places and can be different sizes and colours. Most adult frogs have bulging eyes and **webbed** back feet.

A frog's life story

Like all other animals, a frog goes through different stages as it grows into an adult. These stages make up the animal's life story.

adult

young

We are going to follow the life story of a frog, and watch it change in unusual ways as it develops and grows.

It starts with an egg

A frog starts its life as an egg. The egg is soft and covered with a jelly-like coating. The eggs are known as **frogspawn.**

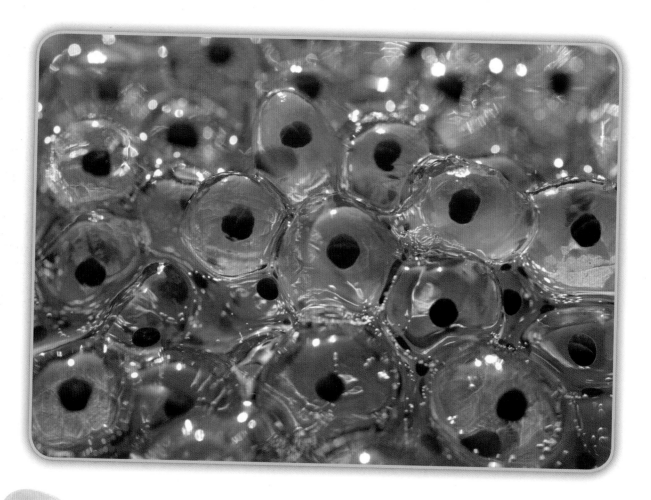

A female frog lays its eggs in water. It lays
many eggs together. Some of them will be
eaten by fish or other animals, but some eggs
survive and hatch.

The egg hatches

Inside the egg is a tiny, dark dot. It eats the jelly surrounding it and grows until it is ready to hatch as a frog **larva.**

A hatched frog larva is called a **tadpole**.
It pushes its way out of the egg and swims
away. It has a rounded body and a long,
flat tail.

The tadpole changes

A tadpole has body parts that help it live underwater. Its tail helps it to swim. It has **gills** that let it breathe underwater.

A tadpole eats weeds under the water.
The food helps the tadpole grow and
change. This change of body shape is called
metamorphosis. Then the tadpole will start to
eat other animals instead of plants.

Changing into a froglet

As the tadpole gets bigger, it changes into a froglet. Now it has front feet and a much smaller tail. It is starting to look more like an adult frog.

The froglet loses its gills and can breathe air with its lungs. When only a very small tail is left, the froglet leaves the water.

Changing into an adult

An adult frog mainly lives on land, but it can still swim in water. Its back feet are webbed to help it swim quickly. The webbing pushes it through the water more strongly.

A frog's back legs are also long and strong to help it jump on land. Its skin is smooth and moist. It can breathe through its skin as well as its lungs.

Some frogs live near ponds or in long damp grass. They are a light brownish colour. This can help to **camouflage** it so other animals can't find and eat them.

poison dart frog

Other frogs live in trees. They have special toes to help them climb. Some frogs can be brightly coloured. Often this means there is poison in their skin.

Frog food

An adult frog eats insects, worms, and slugs. It uses its long tongue to catch **prey**. The tongue lies rolled up in the frog's mouth until the frog sees prey moving. Then it shoots out its sticky tongue to catch its prey.

prey

Some frogs have small teeth that grip prey before they swallow it. They do not use teeth to chew food. Other frogs push food into their mouths using their front feet.

Mating

A frog looks for a mate so it can continue the life story. Together a male and female can **reproduce** and create new frogs. Most frogs mate in the water.

Many male frogs help a female find them by making croaking sounds. Some frogs have skin on their throats that fills with air as they croak.

After mating, the female frog lays eggs.
She lays the eggs in water in springtime
when the water is warmer.

Some female frogs leave their eggs when they are laid. Other **species** of frogs stay with their eggs and take care of them.

A frog's life

A frog **hibernates** in the winter. The frog buries itself into mud or underground to stay warm over the winter months. When spring comes, it comes out again.

Many frogs are eaten by other **predators**, such as birds, snakes, and small **mammals**. However, adult frogs that avoid predators can live for several years.

Frog life story diagram

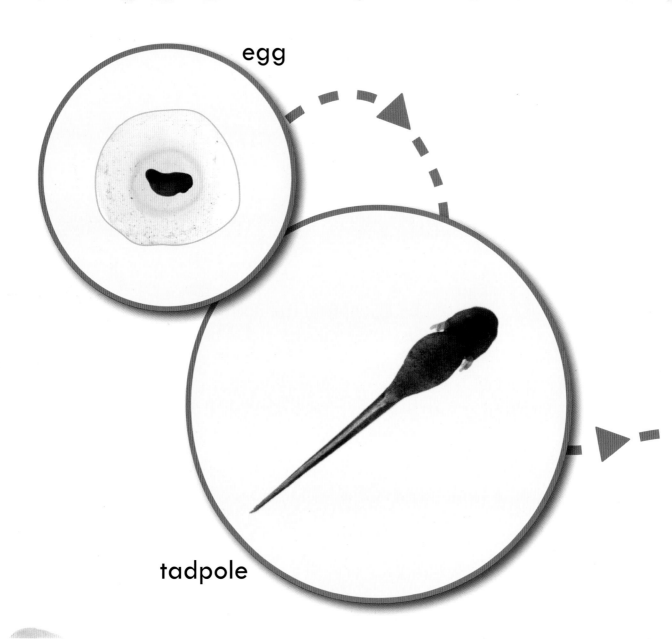

egg

tadpole

adult frog

froglet

Glossary

amphibian animal that can live on land and in water

camouflage skin colour and texture that blends in with the surroundings

frogspawn clump of frog's eggs

gills body parts that animals use to breathe underwater

hibernate spend the winter resting or sleeping

larva stage in an animal's life before it becomes an adult

mammal warm-blooded animal with hair on its body

metamorphosis stages where an animal changes body shape and appearance

predator animal that hunts and eats other animals

prey creature an animal hunts and kills for food

reproduce to lay eggs or give birth to young

species name for a type of living thing

tadpole stage in a frog's development after it is an egg and before it becomes an adult

webbed with flaps of skin stretched between the toes

Find out more

Books

Frog, Ruth Thomson (Wayland, 2013)

Once There Was a Tadpole, Judith Anderson (Wayland, 2012)

Tadpoles and Frogs, Thea Feldman (Kingfisher Books, 2013)

Apps

Rounds: Franklin Frog, Barry and Emma Tranter (Nosy Crow, 2012)

Websites

http://www.bbc.co.uk/nature/life/Frog
Visit the BBC Nature website to find out more about frogs and watch video clips.

http://kids.nationalgeographic.com/kids/animals/creaturefeature/
Click on "amphibians" on the website.

Index